Cubes

Written by Sandra Iversen

Look at these lumps of sugar.
They are cubes.
Cubes have six sides.
The sides are called faces.
The faces are all the same size.

sugar lump

face

3

Look at these boxes.
Some have six sides.
Some have six faces.
But they are not all cubes.
The faces of a cube
are all the same size.

cube-shaped boxes

box

5

These are little cubes.
Do you know some things
that are little cubes like these?

cube

7

These cubes are all candies.
Do you know some candies
that are cubes?

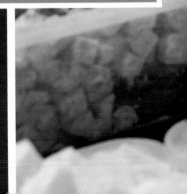

cube-shaped candy

You can make a cube.
You draw a net.
You cut it out.
You fold it up.
All the faces are the same size.

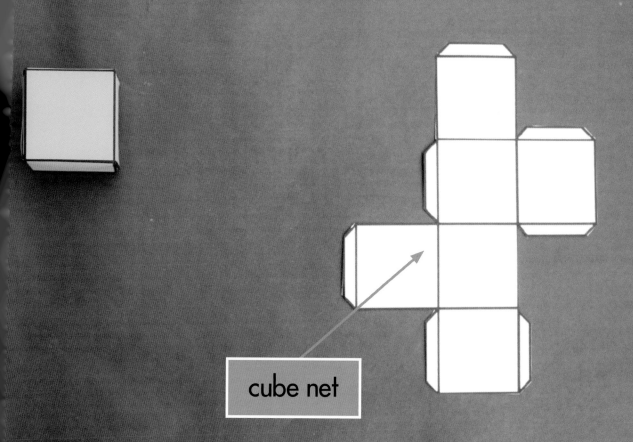

cube net

Make a Cube

draw it

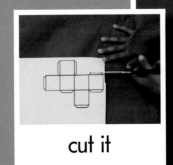
cut it

fold it

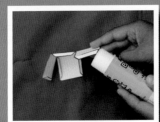
stick it

a cube